It's good to get in touch with you at last.

SABINE

Thank you for your exotic postcard. Forgive me if it is a memory lapse on my part, but should I know you?

GRIFFIN

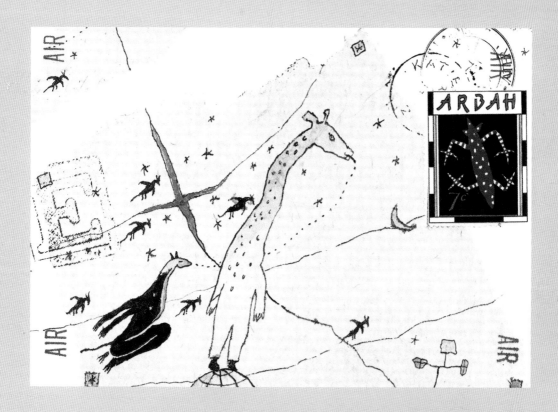

You're right. I am being mysterious but I assure you it's for good reason. . . . I share your sight. When you draw and paint, I see what you're doing while you do it.

SABINE

This is impossible yet it must be true . . . you really can see me can't you?

GRIFFIN

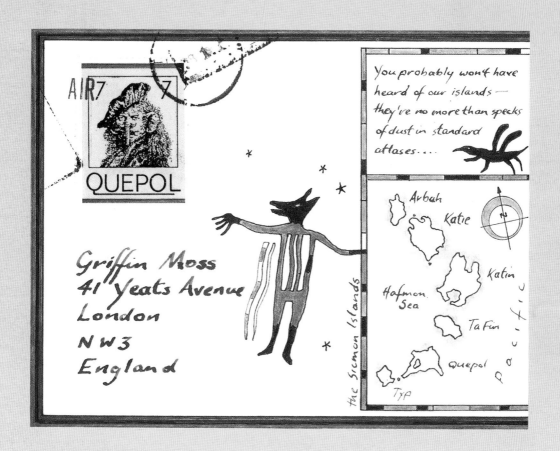

Please don't feel invaded—it's not like that, I promise. But I am impatient to hear about you. Write soon.

SABINE

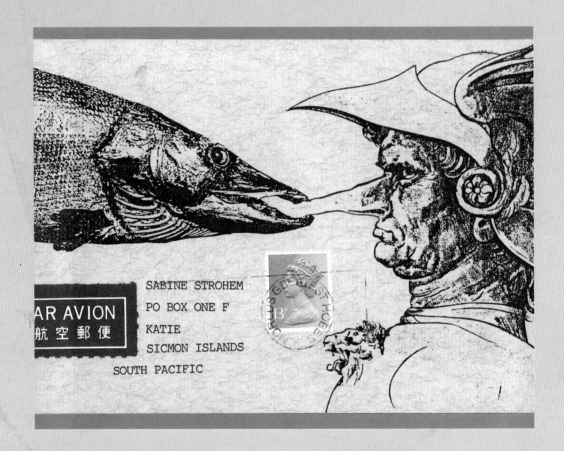

SABINE STROHEM
PO BOX ONE F
KATIE
SICMON ISLANDS
SOUTH PACIFIC

I presume you can't see my writing as well as my pictures, or posting this letter would be superfluous.

Any idea why it's only my images you see?

GRIFFIN

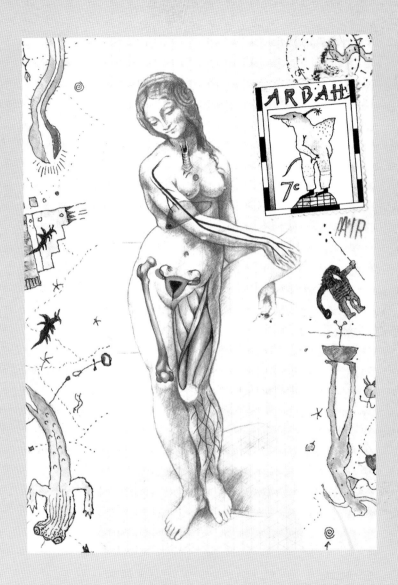

I read your letter again nodding to myself as the events in your life matched
my memory of the way you were painting. . .hearing that my existence
eased your pain made my heart race.

SABINE

I cheer myself by daydreaming of you and the South Seas.

GRIFFIN

Why do I only see your images and not your writing? Because we dream in pictures and not words?
SABINE

SABINE STROHEM
PO BOX ONE F
KATIE
SICMON ISLANDS
SOUTH PACIFIC

VIA AIR MAIL

It's only your cards and letters that keep me going . . . how strange to have a paper love.
GRIFFIN

So you've been making love to me ten thousand miles away—how tantalizing. It accounts for the extreme potency of those drawings.
I'll have to find a way to return the affection.

SABINE

When you found me, I thought my loneliness had gone for good. I was kidding myself. I desperately desire your company.
GRIFFIN

Island magic works on island souls. You and I will heal each other.

SABINE

My days are barren but my nights are heady with you. I want to know what you look like. Will you send a photograph?

GRIFFIN

A photograph would not be possible. If you wish to see me, why not come here? What is there to stop you—you're clearly unhappy where you are. Come.

SABINE

Things have become so difficult. I mustn't write again. Sabine, you don't exist. I invented you . . . before it takes me over it has to stop.

GRIFFIN

You cannot turn me into a phantom because you are frightened. You do not dismiss a muse at whim. If you will not join me, then I shall come to you.

SABINE

If you are reading this, then you exist . . .will you wait for me, be my guest and live here till I return? I'm running from you, but I'm also searching for a way to accept my fate, which I know will be bound to yours. . .
GRIFFIN

MAY

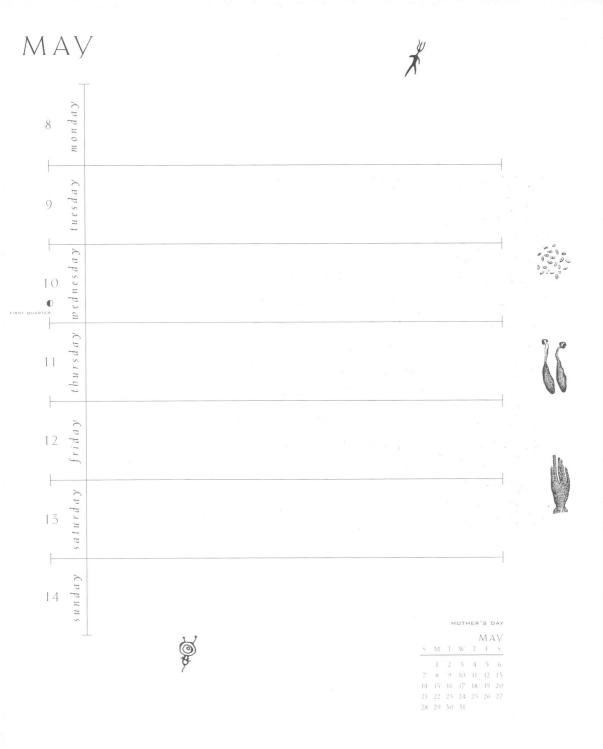

8 monday

9 tuesday

10 wednesday

FIRST QUARTER

11 thursday

12 friday

13 saturday

14 sunday

MAY

S	M	T	W	T	F	S
		1	2	3	4	5	6
7	8	9	10	11	12	13
14	15	16	17	18	19	20
21	22	23	24	25	26	27
28	29	30	31			

MAY

15 monday

16 tuesday

17 wednesday

18 thursday

FULL MOON

19 friday

20 saturday

21 sunday

MAY

S	M	T	W	T	F	S
	1	2	3	4	5	6
7	8	9	10	11	12	13
14	15	16	17	18	19	20
21	22	23	24	25	26	27
28	29	30	31			

I like your house and will be more than content to stay here . . . waiting all those years to find out who you were has prepared me for this; a little more waiting will do me no harm.

SABINE

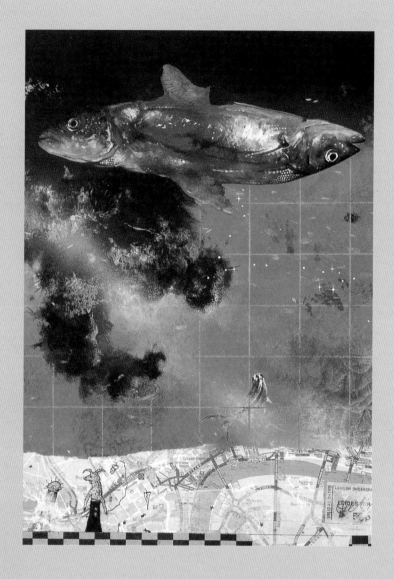

Tomorrow I fly to Florence. . . please write to me.

GRIFFIN

MAY

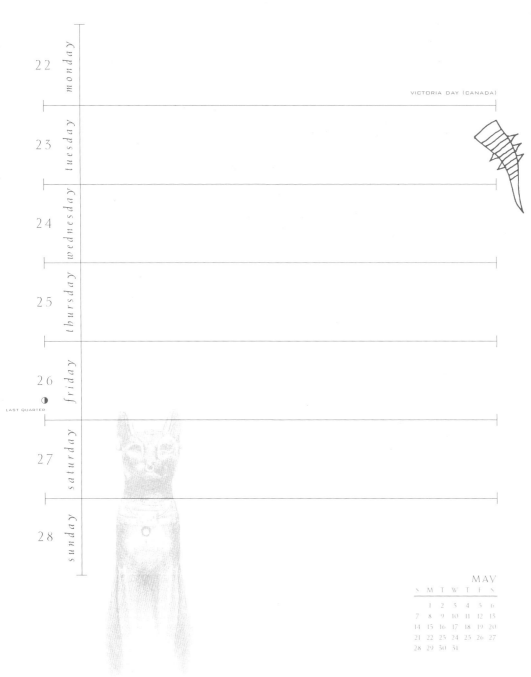

22 *monday*

VICTORIA DAY (CANADA)

23 *tuesday*

24 *wednesday*

25 *thursday*

26 *friday*

LAST QUARTER

27 *saturday*

28 *sunday*

MAY

S	M	T	W	T	F	S
	1	2	3	4	5	6
7	8	9	10	11	12	13
14	15	16	17	18	19	20
21	22	23	24	25	26	27
28	29	30	31			

MAY | JUNE

29 monday

MEMORIAL DAY OBSERVED

30 tuesday

MEMORIAL DAY

31 wednesday

1 thursday

2 friday

NEW MOON

3 saturday

4 sunday

I saw you painting last night, a woman in mist. It brought you close to me.

SABINE

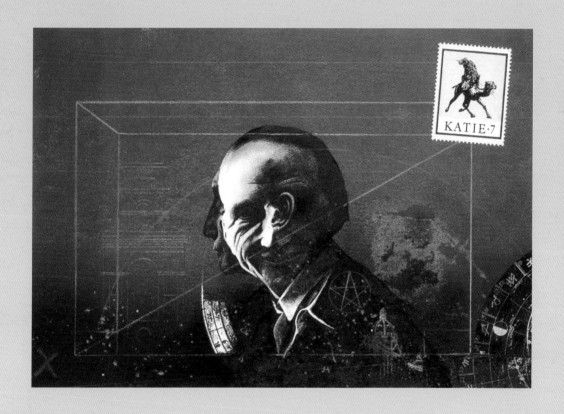

I had a wonderful, sensuous dream last night . . .

GRIFFIN

Italy suits you my love. But be a little cautious; the eye of the storm is a deceptive place.

SABINE

You were right again. . . I need to hold your hand.

GRIFFIN

JUNE

19 *monday*

20 *tuesday*

SOLSTICE

21 *wednesday*

22 *thursday*

23 *friday*

24 *saturday*

LAST QUARTER

25 *sunday*

JUNE

S	M	T	W	T	F	S
				1	2	3
4	5	6	7	8	9	10
11	12	13	14	15	16	17
18	19	20	21	22	23	24
25	26	27	28	29	30	

JUNE|JULY

26 monday

27 tuesday

28 wednesday

29 thursday

30 friday

1 saturday

NEW MOON ●

CANADA DAY

2 sunday

JUNE
S M T W T F S
1 2 3
4 5 6 7 8 9 10
11 12 13 14 15 16 17
18 19 20 21 22 23 24
25 26 27 28 29 30

JULY
S M T W T F S
1
2 3 4 5 6 7 8
9 10 11 12 13 14 15
16 17 18 19 20 21 22
23 24 25 26 27 28 29
30 31

SABINE STROHEM
41 YEATS AV
LONDON NW3
ENGLAND

Why not try to view the next stage of your journey as a transition? Choose reassuring thoughts. Remember, I'm holding the string end and won't allow you to disappear into oblivion . .

SABINE

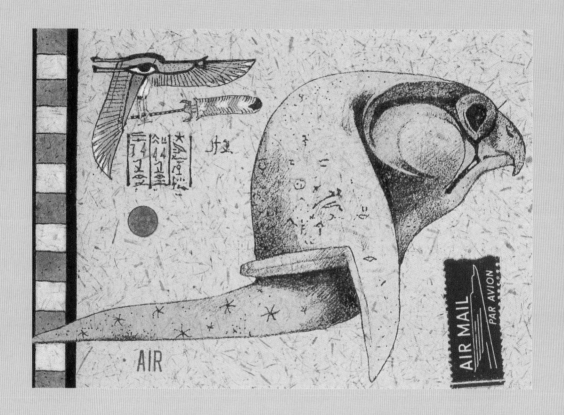

I love you. Please notice I'm choosing reassuring thoughts.

GRIFFIN

I've been drawing in the museum's Egyptian gallery. The silent stones fill me with awe...

SABINE

If I could draw the way I feel about you, I would.
GRIFFIN

Maybe if you were here I wouldn't want.

SABINE

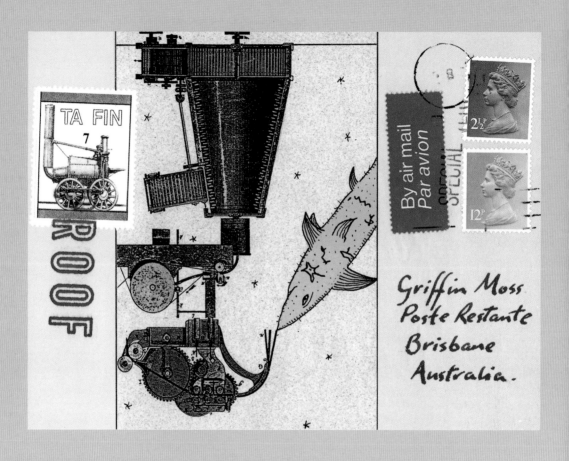

Can you still see me? Will pass through Brisbane. Write there.

GRIFFIN

The openness of your love overwhelms me.

GRIFFIN

Bring yourself home to me and I will immerse you in every ounce of tenderness I possess.

SABINE

AIR MAIL

CHECKED

SABINE STROHEM
41 YEATS AV.
LONDON NW3
ENGLAND

Beware such things as abrupt changes of weather and never underestimate the sea.

SABINE

Two days out from the Solomons, we were hit by a freak wave and I was catapulted overboard . . . when I came to, I was on the boat and the captain was pumping my chest (it was he who hauled me aboard, but it was you who saved me.)

GRIFFIN

AUGUST | SEPTEMBER

28 *monday*

29 *tuesday*

● NEW MOON

30 *wednesday*

31 *thursday*

1 *friday*

2 *saturday*

3 *sunday*

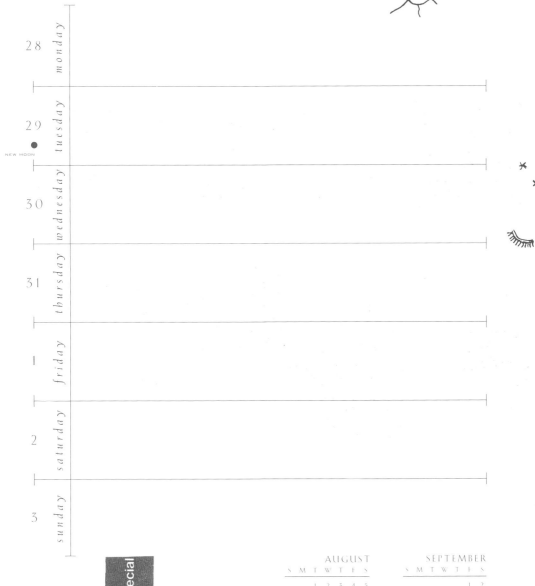

Special

AUGUST
S	M	T	W	T	F	S
		1	2	3	4	5
6	7	8	9	10	11	12
13	14	15	16	17	18	19
20	21	22	23	24	25	26
27	28	29	30	31		

SEPTEMBER
S	M	T	W	T	F	S
					1	2
3	4	5	6	7	8	9
10	11	12	13	14	15	16
17	18	19	20	21	22	23
24	25	26	27	28	29	30

SEPTEMBER

4 monday

LABOR DAY

5 tuesday

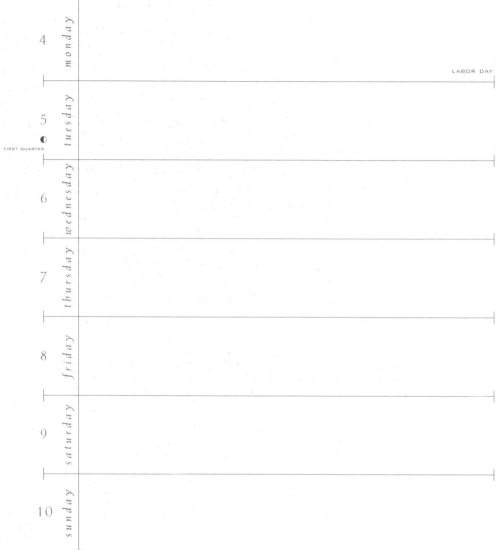

FIRST QUARTER

6 wednesday

7 thursday

8 friday

9 saturday

20
21

10 sunday

SEPTEMBER
S M T W T F S
            1 2
3 4 5 6 7 8 9
10 11 12 13 14 15 16
17 18 19 20 21 22 23
24 25 26 27 28 29 30

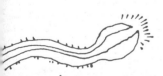

You have survived. Are you coming home when your strength returns? Will I see you at last?

SABINE

I know who you are, what we are, and what we will be to one another. I will be home on the 23rd.

GRIFFIN

I waited but you did not return on the 23rd. What happened? Where are you?

SABINE

You were not here when I returned and there was no sign that you had ever been here. . . I am bewildered. I need you badly.

GRIFFIN

SEPTEMBER | OCTOBER

25   *monday*

26   *tuesday*

27   *wednesday*

NEW MOON ●

28   *thursday*

29   *friday*

30   *saturday*

ROSH HASHANAH

1   *sunday*

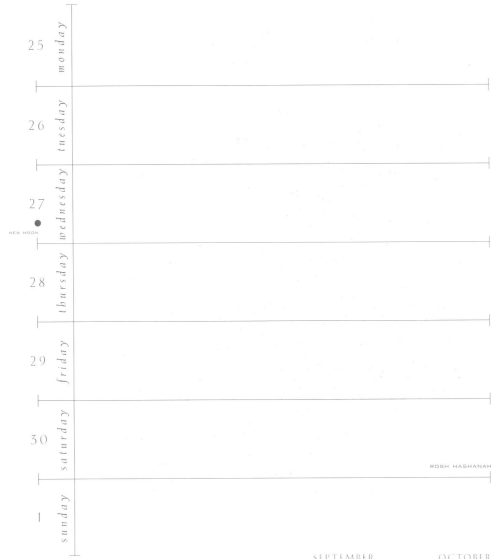

SEPTEMBER
S	M	T	W	T	F	S
					1	2
3	4	5	6	7	8	9
10	11	12	13	14	15	16
17	18	19	20	21	22	23
24	25	26	27	28	29	30

OCTOBER
S	M	T	W	T	F	S
1	2	3	4	5	6	7
8	9	10	11	12	13	14
15	16	17	18	19	20	21
22	23	24	25	26	27	28
29	30	31				

AIR PAR AVION MAIL

OCTOBER

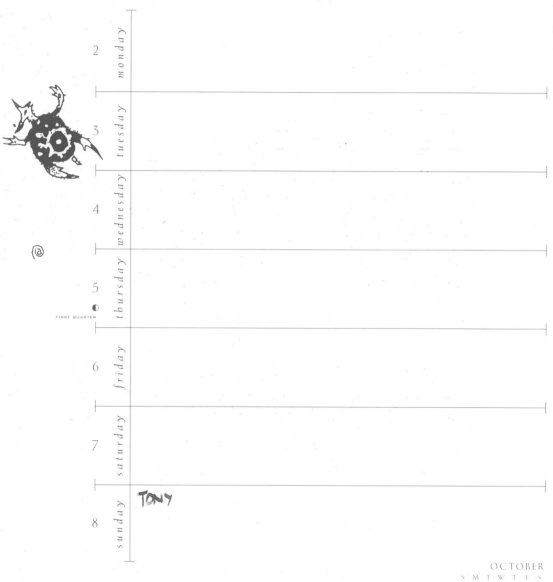

2   monday

3   tuesday

4   wednesday

5   thursday

FIRST QUARTER

6   friday

7   saturday

8   sunday   TONY

OCTOBER

S	M	T	W	T	F	S
1	2	3	4	5	6	7
8	9	10	11	12	13	14
15	16	17	18	19	20	21
22	23	24	25	26	27	28
29	30	31				

I am frustrated at not being able to hold you in my arms; I feel like I'm being teased by an unseen adversary.

SABINE

This overlapping of time and space seems like we're living in parallel universes. Do you think we are separated for life, unable to exist in each other's presence?

GRIFFIN

OCTOBER

9 *monday*	
	YOM KIPPUR
	COLUMBUS DAY OBSERVED
	CANADIAN THANKSGIVING
10 *tuesday*	
11 *wednesday*	
12 *thursday*	
	COLUMBUS DAY
13 *friday* ○	
FULL MOON	
14 *saturday*	
15 *sunday*	

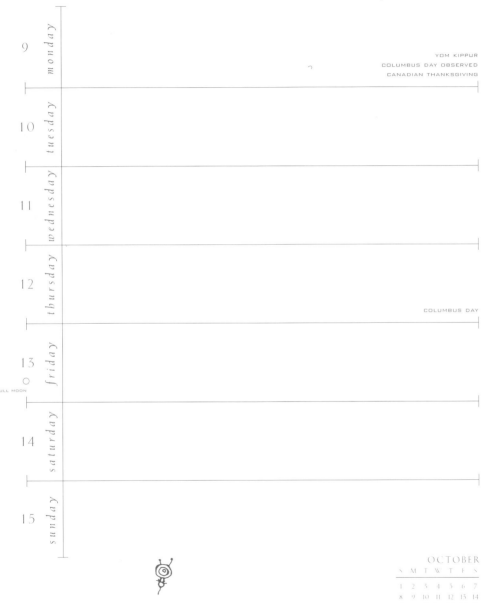

OCTOBER

S M T W T F S

1 2 3 4 5 6 7
8 9 10 11 12 13 14
15 16 17 18 19 20 21
22 23 24 25 26 27 28
29 30 31

OCTOBER

16 *monday*

17 *tuesday*

18 *wednesday*

19 *thursday*

20 *friday*

LAST QUARTER

21 *saturday*

22 *sunday*

OCTOBER

S	M	T	W	T	F	S
1	2	3	4	5	6	7
8	9	10	11	12	13	14
15	16	17	18	19	20	21
22	23	24	25	26	27	28
29	30	31				

I think that the concept of parallel universes is too grand. This I sense is a more personal test of our tenacity. If we solve our problem, we gain the reward of each other.

SABINE

ceremonial
spinning top

I'd never experienced real desire till you arrived . . . we must find a way to be together or I will combust.

GRIFFIN

OCTOBER

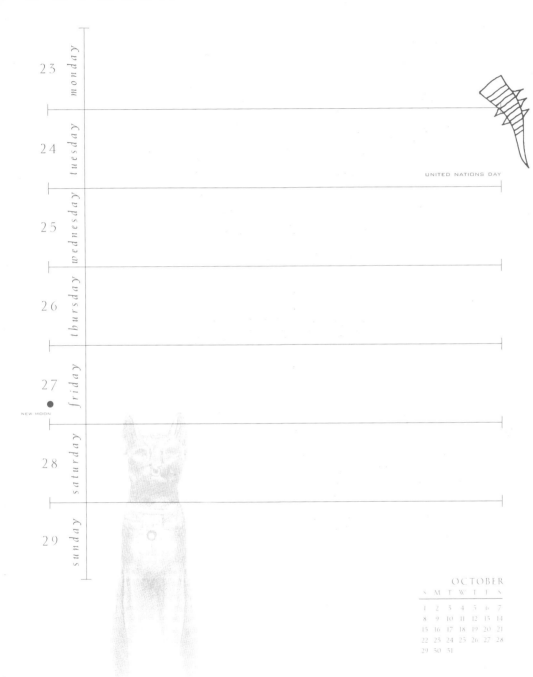

23 monday

24 tuesday

UNITED NATIONS DAY

25 wednesday

26 thursday

27 friday

NEW MOON

28 saturday

29 sunday

OCTOBER

S	M	T	W	T	F	S
1	2	3	4	5	6	7
8	9	10	11	12	13	14
15	16	17	18	19	20	21
22	23	24	25	26	27	28
29	30	31				

OCTOBER|NOVEMBER

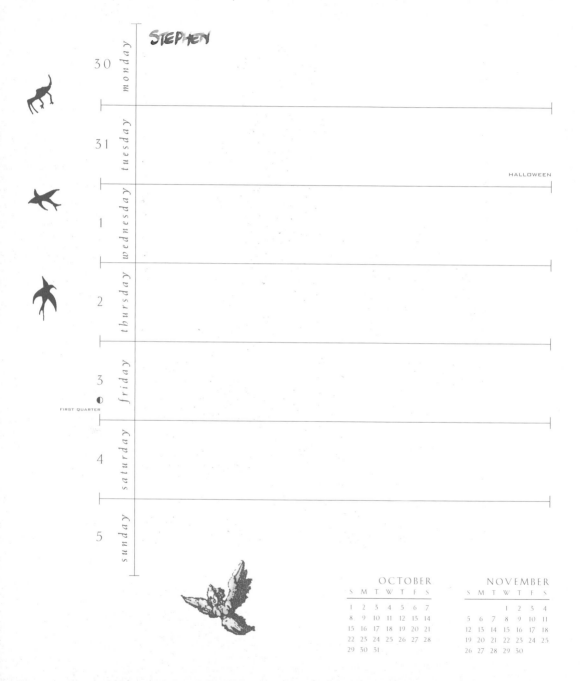

30 monday — STEPHEN

31 tuesday — HALLOWEEN

1 wednesday

2 thursday

3 friday — FIRST QUARTER

4 saturday

5 sunday

OCTOBER
S M T W T F S
1 2 3 4 5 6 7
8 9 10 11 12 13 14
15 16 17 18 19 20 21
22 23 24 25 26 27 28
29 30 31

NOVEMBER
S M T W T F S
1 2 3 4
5 6 7 8 9 10 11
12 13 14 15 16 17 18
19 20 21 22 23 24 25
26 27 28 29 30

Being apart from you is unbearable.

SABINE

7 PORT-LOUIS — Escalier des Rochers Sculptès. — LL.

We have to do something. If I can't reach your world and you can't be in mine while I'm here, maybe there's another place halfway . . .

GRIFFIN

NOVEMBER

CARL

6 monday

7 tuesday

ELECTION DAY

8 wednesday

9 thursday

10 friday

11
○
FULL MOON
saturday

VETERANS DAY
REMEMBRANCE DAY (CANADA)

12 sunday

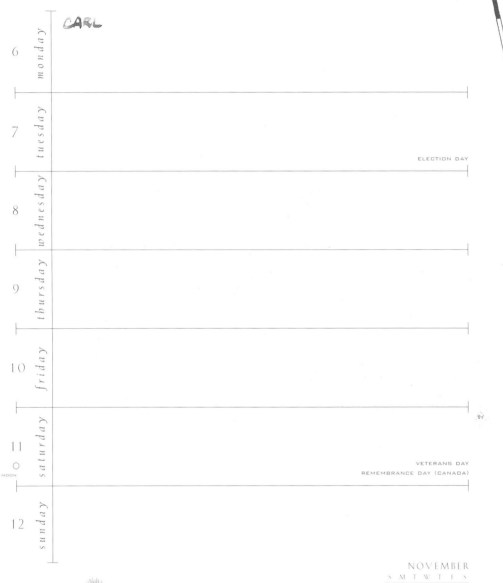

NOVEMBER

S	M	T	W	T	F	S
			1	2	3	4
5	6	7	8	9	10	11
12	13	14	15	16	17	18
19	20	21	22	23	24	25
26	27	28	29	30		

from J Griffin wombils in
Flood the Hermetic

NOVEMBER

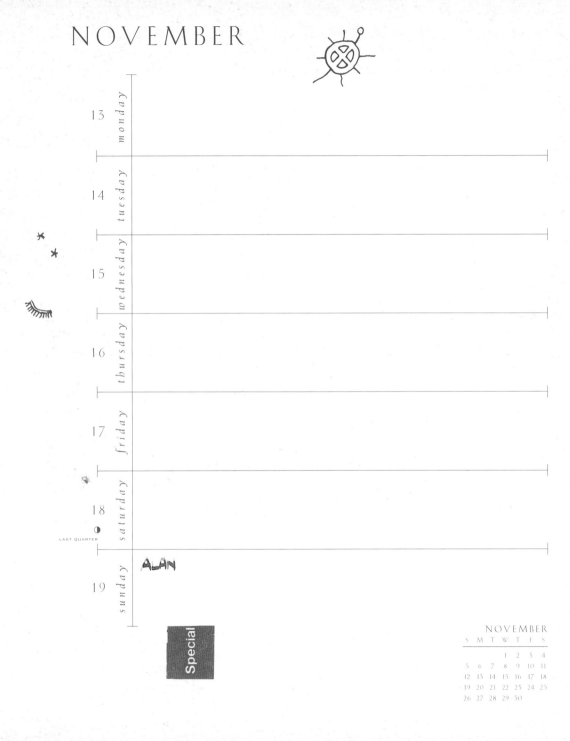

13 monday

14 tuesday

15 wednesday

16 thursday

17 friday

18 saturday

LAST QUARTER

19 sunday

ALAN

Special

NOVEMBER
S M T W T F S
1 2 3 4
5 6 7 8 9 10 11
12 13 14 15 16 17 18
19 20 21 22 23 24 25
26 27 28 29 30

Perhaps Alexandria is the place where we could meet. Perhaps the gate will let us both pass through. Will you meet me there?

SABINE

Griffin Moss
17 Cott Cottages
Dartington
Devon England

AIR MAIL

What you suggest is crazy, simplistic and impossible.
GRIFFIN

NOVEMBER

20	*monday*
21	*tuesday*
22	*wednesday*
23	*thursday*
24	*friday*
25	*saturday*
26	*sunday*

THANKSGIVING

NEW MOON

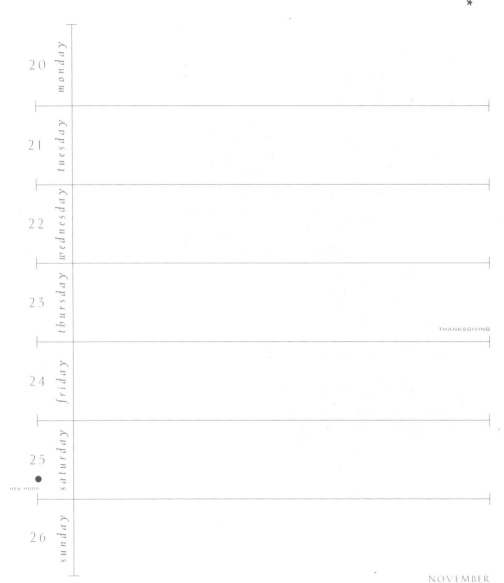

NOVEMBER

S	M	T	W	T	F	S
			1	2	3	4
5	6	7	8	9	10	11
12	13	14	15	16	17	18
19	20	21	22	23	24	25
26	27	28	29	30		

NOVEMBER | DECEMBER

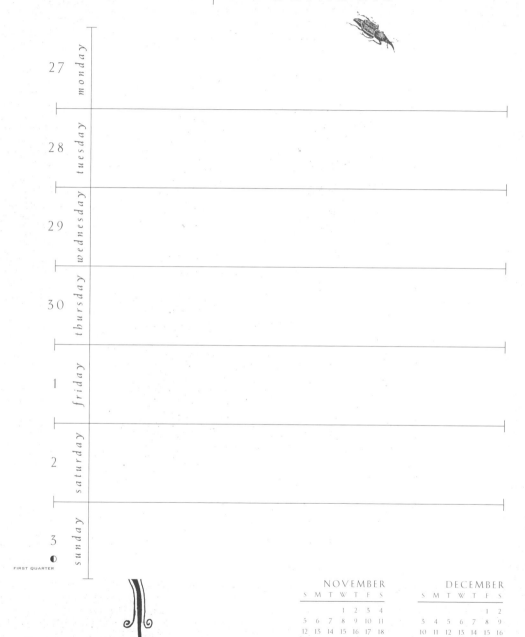

27 *monday*

28 *tuesday*

29 *wednesday*

30 *thursday*

1 *friday*

2 *saturday*

3 *sunday*

● FIRST QUARTER

NOVEMBER
S M T W T F S
            1 2 3 4
5 6 7 8 9 10 11
12 13 14 15 16 17 18
19 20 21 22 23 24 25
26 27 28 29 30

DECEMBER
S M T W T F S
                  1 2
3 4 5 6 7 8 9
10 11 12 13 14 15 16
17 18 19 20 21 22 23
24 25 26 27 28 29 30
31

Will you leave everything behind so that we can be together?

SABINE

But of course I will meet you. There is no reason without you.

GRIFFIN

Do not hesitate my love.

SABINE

Mail Par avion

SABINE STROHEM
PO BOX ONE F
KATIE
SICMON ISLANDS
SOUTH PACIFIC

I will be at the Pharos in Alexandria on the 21st. I trust you know we shall be together.

GRIFFIN

I am filled with so much hope.

SABINE

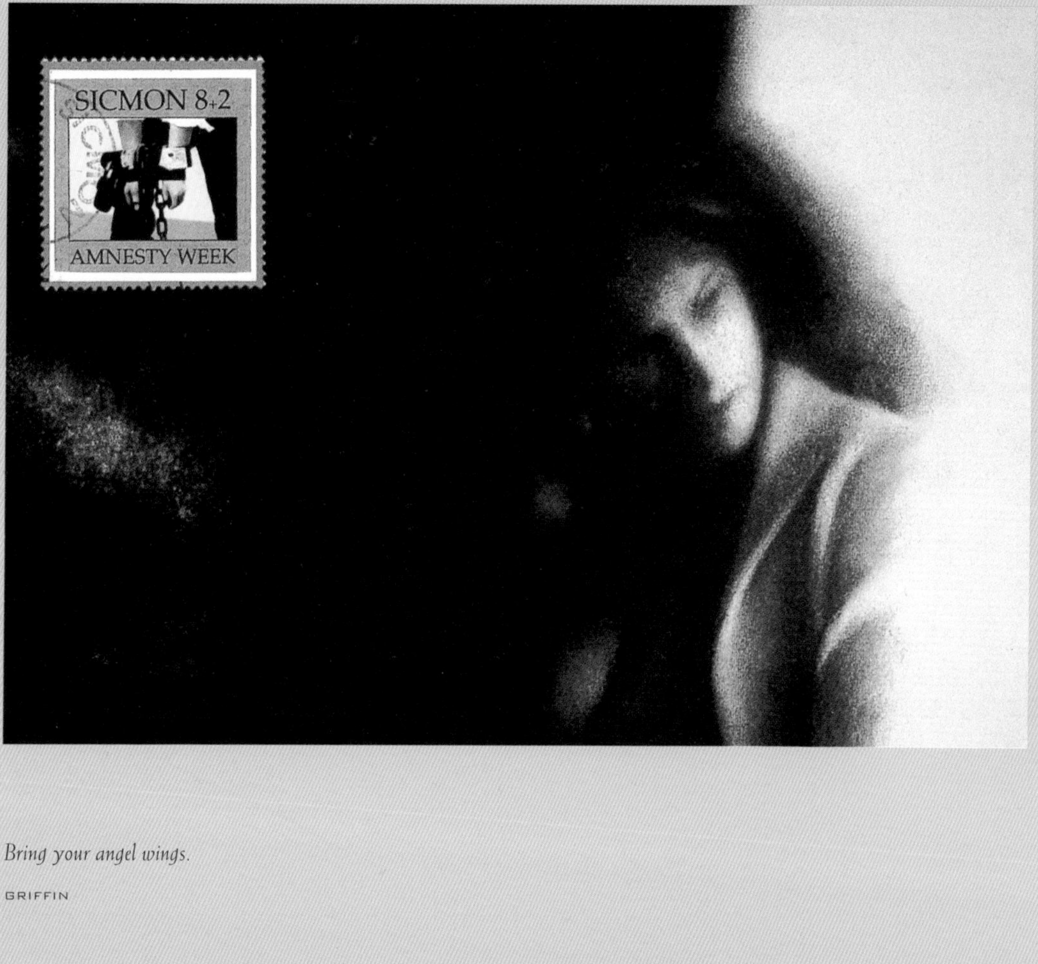
SICMON 8+2
AMNESTY WEEK

Bring your angel wings.

GRIFFIN

NOTES

NOTES

SPECIAL DATES

1999

JANUARY	FEBRUARY	MARCH	APRIL	MAY	JUNE

S M T W T F S	S M T W T F S	S M T W T F S	S M T W T F S	S M T W T F S	S M T W T F S
1 2	1 2 3 4 5 6	1 2 3 4 5 6	1 2 3	1	1 2 3 4 5
3 4 5 6 7 8 9	7 8 9 10 11 12 13	7 8 9 10 11 12 13	4 5 6 7 8 9 10	2 3 4 5 6 7 8	6 7 8 9 10 11 12
10 11 12 13 14 15 16	14 15 16 17 18 19 20	14 15 16 17 18 19 20	11 12 13 14 15 16 17	9 10 11 12 13 14 15	13 14 15 16 17 18 19
17 18 19 20 21 22 23	21 22 23 24 25 26 27	21 22 23 24 25 26 27	18 19 20 21 22 23 24	16 17 18 19 20 21 22	20 21 22 23 24 25 26
24 25 26 27 28 29 30	28	28 29 30 31	25 26 27 28 29 30	23 24 25 26 27 28 29	27 28 29 30
31				30 31	

JULY	AUGUST	SEPTEMBER	OCTOBER	NOVEMBER	DECEMBER

S M T W T F S	S M T W T F S	S M T W T F S	S M T W T F S	S M T W T F S	S M T W T F S
1 2 3	1 2 3 4 5 6 7	1 2 3 4	1 2	1 2 3 4 5 6	1 2 3 4
4 5 6 7 8 9 10	8 9 10 11 12 13 14	5 6 7 8 9 10 11	3 4 5 6 7 8 9	7 8 9 10 11 12 13	5 6 7 8 9 10 11
11 12 13 14 15 16 17	15 16 17 18 19 20 21	12 13 14 15 16 17 18	10 11 12 13 14 15 16	14 15 16 17 18 19 20	12 13 14 15 16 17 18
18 19 20 21 22 23 24	22 23 24 25 26 27 28	19 20 21 22 23 24 25	17 18 19 20 21 22 23	21 22 23 24 25 26 27	19 20 21 22 23 24 25
25 26 27 28 29 30 31	29 30 31	26 27 28 29 30	24 25 26 27 28 29 30	28 29 30	26 27 28 29 30 31
			31		

2000

JANUARY	FEBRUARY	MARCH	APRIL	MAY	JUNE

S M T W T F S	S M T W T F S	S M T W T F S	S M T W T F S	S M T W T F S	S M T W T F S
1	1 2 3 4 5	1 2 3 4	1	1 2 3 4 5 6	1 2 3
2 3 4 5 6 7 8	6 7 8 9 10 11 12	5 6 7 8 9 10 11	2 3 4 5 6 7 8	7 8 9 10 11 12 13	4 5 6 7 8 9 10
9 10 11 12 13 14 15	13 14 15 16 17 18 19	12 13 14 15 16 17 18	9 10 11 12 13 14 15	14 15 16 17 18 19 20	11 12 13 14 15 16 17
16 17 18 19 20 21 22	20 21 22 23 24 25 26	19 20 21 22 23 24 25	16 17 18 19 20 21 22	21 22 23 24 25 26 27	18 19 20 21 22 23 24
23 24 25 26 27 28 29	27 28 29	26 27 28 29 30 31	23 24 25 26 27 28 29	28 29 30 31	25 26 27 28 29 30
30 31			30		

JULY	AUGUST	SEPTEMBER	OCTOBER	NOVEMBER	DECEMBER

S M T W T F S	S M T W T F S	S M T W T F S	S M T W T F S	S M T W T F S	S M T W T F S
1	1 2 3 4 5	1 2	1 2 3 4 5 6 7	1 2 3 4	1 2
2 3 4 5 6 7 8	6 7 8 9 10 11 12	3 4 5 6 7 8 9	8 9 10 11 12 13 14	5 6 7 8 9 10 11	3 4 5 6 7 8 9
9 10 11 12 13 14 15	13 14 15 16 17 18 19	10 11 12 13 14 15 16	15 16 17 18 19 20 21	12 13 14 15 16 17 18	10 11 12 13 14 15 16
16 17 18 19 20 21 22	20 21 22 23 24 25 26	17 18 19 20 21 22 23	22 23 24 25 26 27 28	19 20 21 22 23 24 25	17 18 19 20 21 22 23
23 24 25 26 27 28 29	27 28 29 30 31	24 25 26 27 28 29 30	29 30 31	26 27 28 29 30	24 25 26 27 28 29 30
30 31					31

2001

JANUARY	FEBRUARY	MARCH	APRIL	MAY	JUNE

S M T W T F S	S M T W T F S	S M T W T F S	S M T W T F S	S M T W T F S	S M T W T F S
1 2 3 4 5 6	1 2 3	1 2 3	1 2 3 4 5 6 7	1 2 3 4 5	1 2
7 8 9 10 11 12 13	4 5 6 7 8 9 10	4 5 6 7 8 9 10	8 9 10 11 12 13 14	6 7 8 9 10 11 12	3 4 5 6 7 8 9
14 15 16 17 18 19 20	11 12 13 14 15 16 17	11 12 13 14 15 16 17	15 16 17 18 19 20 21	13 14 15 16 17 18 19	10 11 12 13 14 15 16
21 22 23 24 25 26 27	18 19 20 21 22 23 24	18 19 20 21 22 23 24	22 23 24 25 26 27 28	20 21 22 23 24 25 26	17 18 19 20 21 22 23
28 29 30 31	25 26 27 28	25 26 27 28 29 30 31	29 30	27 28 29 30 31	24 25 26 27 28 29 30

JULY	AUGUST	SEPTEMBER	OCTOBER	NOVEMBER	DECEMBER

S M T W T F S	S M T W T F S	S M T W T F S	S M T W T F S	S M T W T F S	S M T W T F S
1 2 3 4 5 6 7	1 2 3 4	1	1 2 3 4 5 6	1 2 3	1
8 9 10 11 12 13 14	5 6 7 8 9 10 11	2 3 4 5 6 7 8	7 8 9 10 11 12 13	4 5 6 7 8 9 10	2 3 4 5 6 7 8
15 16 17 18 19 20 21	12 13 14 15 16 17 18	9 10 11 12 13 14 15	14 15 16 17 18 19 20	11 12 13 14 15 16 17	9 10 11 12 13 14 15
22 23 24 25 26 27 28	19 20 21 22 23 24 25	16 17 18 19 20 21 22	21 22 23 24 25 26 27	18 19 20 21 22 23 24	16 17 18 19 20 21 22
29 30 31	26 27 28 29 30 31	23 24 25 26 27 28 29	28 29 30 31	25 26 27 28 29 30	23 24 25 26 27 28 29
		30			30 31